Supreme Sa...
Other Moral Tales
from
MAHABHARATHA

By

Kolar Krishna Iyer

FIRST EDITION
An imprint of Sura Books (Pvt) Ltd.
(An ISO 9001:2000 Certified Company)
Chennai • Tirunelveli • Ernakulam
Palakkad • Thiruvananthapuram • Bengalooru

Price : ₹55.00

© PUBLISHERS

SUPREME SACRIFICE AND OTHER MORAL TALES FROM MAHABHARATHA

by Kolar Krishna Iyer

This Edition	:	March, 2012
Size	:	1/8 Crown
Pages	:	112
Code No.	:	G 53

Price : ₹ 55.00

ISBN : 81-7478-114-5

[NO ONE IS PERMITTED TO COPY OR TRANSLATE IN ANY OTHER LANGUAGE THE CONTENTS OF THIS BOOK OR PART THEREOF IN ANY FORM WITHOUT THE WRITTEN PERMISSION OF THE PUBLISHERS]

YOUNG KIDS PRESS

[An imprint of Sura Books (Pvt) Ltd.]

Head Office: 1620, 'J' Block, 16th Main Road, Anna Nagar, **Chennai - 600 040.** Phones: 044-26162173, 26161099.

Branches :
- KAP Complex, I Floor, 20, Trivandrum Road, **Tirunelveli - 627 002.** Phone : 0462-4200557
- XXXII/2328, New Kalavath Road, Opp. to BSNL, Near Chennoth Glass, Palarivattom, **Ernakulam - 682 025.** Phones: 0484-3205797, 2535636
- Shop No. 7, Municipal Complex, Robinson Road, **Palakkad - 678 001.** Phone : 0491-2504270
- TC 28/2816, Srinikelan, Kuthiravattam Road, Chirakulam, **Thiruvananthapuram - 695 001.** Phone: 0471-4063864
- 3638/A, IVth Cross, Opp. to Malleswaram Railway Station, Gayathri Nagar, Back gate of Subramaniya Nagar, **Bengalooru - 560 021.** Phone: 080-23324950

Printed at G.T. Krishna Press, Chennai - 600 102 and Published by V.V.K.Subburaj for Young kids press [An imprint of Spura Books (Pvt) Ltd.] 1620, 'J' Block, 16th Main Road, Anna Nagar, Chennai - 600 040. Phones: 26162173, 26161099. Fax: (91) 44-26162173. e-mail: enquiry@surabooks.com; website: www.surabooks.com

Preface

The Epic Mahabharata is full of moral episodes depicting supreme sacrifice, grateful children and woman who make great sacrifices to fulfill the wishes of their parents; episodes depicting the consequences of evil habits like addiction to gambling. They give tips for leading a virtuous life etc. The episode when read by young boys and girls, their minds become dyed to their thoughts, foster their psychological health and induce in them largeness of mind and normative vision. They also give moral contentment. They teach us right spiritual and moral way of life to lead by acquiring spiritual knowledge and become ideal citizens by leading a life of self-sacrifice, adherence to truth, justice, equality, compassion and love towards all living beings irrespective of caste and creed.

The following tales are intended to achieve the above goals by the young and old readers.

Kolar Krishna Iyer

Contents

	Page
1. The Supreme Sacrifice	1
2. Evil of Gambling	8
3. Jealousy	19
4. From Sovereign to Servant	24
5. Yudhishtira and the Yakshadevata Quiz	32
6. The Mouse Girl	40
7. Sarmistha	46
8. Bhargava Rama	52
9. Garuthmantha	66
10. Bhishmacharya	73
11. Bakasura, the Demon	83
12. Ekalavya	93
13. Sibi Chakravarthi	97
14. Lord Vishnu Gives Food	102
15. Dharmavyadha	105

Supreme Sacrifice and Other Moral Tales from Mahabharata

1. The Supreme Sacrifice

After the victory in the Kurukshetra war, Yudhishtira, the Pandava king performed Aswamedha Yaga. Kings from all over the kingdom of Bharata were invited. They all praised the way in which the Yaga was performed with great pomp and gaiety. To the several hundreds of brahmins, poor people and destitutes, Yudhishtira gave by way of charity large sums of money and gifts. All were entertained to sumptuous luncheon and dinner. They said that there was no greater philanthropist than Yudhishtira.

While the Yaga was in progress, a mongoose suddenly appeared in the Yagasala from nowhere. One side of the animal was shining like gold. It stood among those assembled and began to laugh mockingly. Everybody was taken aback with surprise seeing the animal laughing like that. They suspected that it might be a devil that had come to destroy the Yaga. It began to address those assembled thus:

SURA'S ● Supreme Sacrifice and Other Moral Tales from Mahabharata

"Oh great kings and brahmins assembled here, listen. Are you all feeling proud that the king Yudhishtira is performing with such pomp and gaiety and is giving lavishly charity and gifts that has no parallel. This charity given by the king is nothing when compared to what a

poor brahmin once while gave. It was really very great, the present charity now dispensed is insignificant. As such why are you all so elated and praising it so loudly?"

The brahmins were stunned and asked the mongoose:

"Who are you? From where are you coming? Why are you criticising the charity of Yudhishtira, the very embodiment of Dharma, like this. When the Yaga is being performed according to the Sastras and everybody is satisfied, it is not proper on your part to criticise like this."

The mongoose in reply said:

Oh, learned brahmins! There is not even an iota of untruth in what I have said. I am not jealous of Dharmaraja. I reiterate that the charity dispensed by the poor brahmin was far greater than what is being now dispensed here. As a consequence of the charity dispensed by the poor brahmin, he along with his wife, son and daughter-in-law, all found a place in Swargaloka. I was a witness to that. I shall now narrate the episode, please listen.

A poor brahmin was living on alms, before the Kurukshetra war. He was even gathering the grain that had fallen on the ground for their food. His family was sharing that food equally among them. He never used to gather grain more than what was required for that day. Sometimes he could not get any grain at all and on that day they all had to starve. Once famine struck the kingdom. For want of rains there were no agricultural operations. Not a single grain used to be available to the poor brahmin. Some days they used to sustain by drinking water.

One day however he was lucky enough to procure one measure of maize. They converted it into flour and were about to share it for their lunch that afternoon. Just then a brahmin came with hunger. He was invited into the house as a guest and to have the afternoon lunch. He told the guest:

"I am a poor brahmin living by begging. Please be satisfied with whatever is available with me and what I offer you."

First the poor brahmin served his share of the flour. This did not abate the hunger of the guest. He craved for some more food. The poor brahmin looked at his wife. She understood the husband's wish and she agreed to part with the flour to the guest most gladly. But, he said to her:

"Even ants get food and serve to their wives and children. I am worse than even ants. I am even snatching away your share of the flour and make you suffer from hunger. What benefit would accrue to me if I make the charity at the expense of another person's suffering?"

She did not agree. She consoled him saying:

"Respected husband, we both are, according to Dharma Sastra, expected to share either good or bad, happiness or sorrow, being couples. So, I am bound to come to your rescue when your honour is at stake. It is our duty to feed a guest to his full satisfaction."

The guest ate that part of the flour also and even then his hunger did not abate. He was looking for more food. Then the son offered his share of the flour to the guest. His father said to him:

"Beloved son, youth and old people can withstand hunger. But, not children of your age. I am loath to take away even your share of the food and offer it to the guest:

His son consoled his father thus:

"Father, it is the duty of a son to come to the aid of his old father when he is discharging the Dharma of feeding a guest to his full satisfaction. I am only a part of you, is it not? As such my share of the flour belongs to you also. Satisfy the hunger of the guest."

The guest observed:

"Dear boy, your behaviour makes me feel proud of you. May God bless you."

The guest took the share of the boy also and yet he continued to feel that his hunger has not abated. He looked at the poor brahmin for some flour. The poor brahmin was at a loss as to from where to get more flour. His daughter-in-law seeing the predicament of his father-in-law offered her share of the flour. But, the Brahmin felt that it was very uncharitable to deprive her also of her share of the food when she was also hungry. He said to her:

"If I deprive you of your food, I would be committing a great sin. You are still very young and would not be able to withstand hunger like either me or your mother-in-law."

She however insisted on taking her share saying:

"You are lord to my lord. Master to my master. I am not younger than your son. If you satisfy the hunger of the guest with the share of my flour, I will also reap the benefit of a good act done. So, please take my share of the food and serve it to the hungry guest."

The guest blessed her also. Now his hunger was fully met and looked satisfied. He told them:

"Your charity dispensation today has no parallel in the world. See, Gods are showering flowers on you from the heaven! They, the Devatas and the Gandharvas, have also come from the heaven to personally look at you and bless you. On account of your charity today all your ancestors have also found a place in Swargaloka. People who are hungry lose their moral and Dharma sense but you four though very hungry did not give up the Dharma of feeding a guest to his full satisfaction. The benefit that accrues to persons performing Rajasooya and Aswamedha Yagas is very insignificant compared to the fruit of your charitable act that has accrued to you today. Divine Chariot has arrived to take you all to Swargaloka. God bless you all."

The guest thereafter disappeared from that place. The mongoose continued:

"I was witness to the above happening. The poor brahmin along with his family thus went to Swargaloka. I was very near the place where the poor brahmin had kept the flour. As soon as I smelt the flour, all my head began to shine like gold. I then went and rolled my body on the floor where the flour was kept. As soon as the remnant flour on the floor touched a part of my body, that part also shone like gold. With a view to get my whole body shine like gold I visited several Yagasalas where charity was being dispensed on a large scale. I have now come here where I learn Yudhishtira is dispensing charity in a way unparalleled. But, as you all see my body has not acquired that gold shine to my great disappointment."

"You have all listened to the episode of the poor brahmin and his charity dispensation. The poor brahmin gave away in charity what he and his family absolutely needed for themselves, to sustain their lives while Yudhishtira is dispensing only a part of his wealth which is surplus and without which he and his family members would not suffer in any way. Oh learned brahmins! Now tell which is greater? The charity of the poor brahmin or that of Yudhishtira!"

So saying the mongoose disappeared from there.

2. Evil of Gambling

This episode from Mahabharata teaches us how gambling leads to the down fall of a person however learned and great he is and makes him suffer untold hardship and misery in life. Gamblers are prepared to take everything they possess including their wives. This episode further tells us how the wicked people use all sorts of arguments justifying their evil designs and incite persons to fall a prey to their evil designs.

Dharmaraja, the Pandava king successfully completed the performance of Rajasooya Yaga in Indraprasthanagar. The great sage Vyasa before taking leave of Dharmaraja gave him some advice:

"Son of Kunti, listen! You are destined to face an evil period of thirteen years hereafter. There are indications of the downfall of the Kshatriya clan. As you all think, with death of the demon Sisupala, evil days have not ended. You may have to face difficult days in the near future. Many persons and even kings may have to die. And you will be the person responsible for the evil that will befall on your race! You may have to wage a great war against your cousins in which most of the Kshatriyas would perish. Nobody can alter the destiny! You continue to adhere to Dharma and administer the country."

After the departure of the sage Vyasa. Dharmaraja began to feel agitated. He informed his brothers what the sage Vyasa had told him. He told them:

"Dear brothers, I feel dejected. I don't feel it is no more worth living for me after what the sage had told, especially that I would be the person responsible for the evil things that are to take place!"

Arjuna consoled him saying:

"Brother, you should not feel dejected. You are now the king of kings. Let us face courageously evil events as and when they take place."

"Dear brothers," Dharmaraja continued:

"God alone should save us! We have committed no sin so far. We will not in the future also. I am taking a vow not to do anything that would lead to a conflict. So, let us all discard anger. Let us not do anything against the wishes of our cousin Duryodhana and others to avoid any conflict. Let us be friendly with them all. Let us take a vow to this effect."

"We all agree with you!" assured all his brothers.

This vow taken by him was one of the reasons as to why he could not refuse the invitation to play dice with Duryodhana. But, the consequences of the very vow itself ultimately led to the conflict between the Pandavas and the Kauravas and to the great Kurukshetra war. It was the vow that made Dharmaraja not refuse the invitation to play the game of dice and the consequences of the dice gamble that led to the further events which ended in the great war between the cousins.

This is an example which shows that all man's intelligence, desire and effort sometimes lead to results not contemplated by him. Man proposes and Destiny disposes!

SURA'S ● Supreme Sacrifice and Other Moral Tales from Mahabharata

In Hastinapur, Duryodhana became very jealous of Pandavas after attending the Rajasooya Yaga and seeing the splendour, their wealth, power and their popularity among all the kings.

Sakuni, his uncle, observed the agitated mind of Duryodhana. He enquired him the reason for his worry. Duryodhana told him:

"Dear uncle, supported by his brothers Dharmaraja is living like Devendra in Indraloka. Sisupala was killed in the very presence of all the kings. Yet no king protested. Everybody was afraid of the Pandavas' strength. On the other hand they all showered costly gifts and praises on Dharmaraja. How can I not feel jealous of him and his brothers?"

Sakuni consoled him again:

"Duryodhana! Pandavas are after all your cousins. Why should you feel jealous of their prosperity? They got what was legally due to them and they are enjoying it. Their stars are on the ascendancy! They have earned everything with their own effort. They have not harmed anybody. How are you affected if they are powerful and popular? Your ninetynine brothers are all on your side. They all respect you and support you. Great warriors and leaders like Bheeshmacharya, Krupacharya, Jayadratha, Somadatha, myself and all of us are on your side. Still why are you worried and agitated?"

"If that is so, uncle, with the help of all these persons why can't we wage a war against the Pandavas and annex

Indraprastha kingdom with all their wealth?" asked Duryodhana.

"No.. no.. Duryodhana. This is a very risky proposal. I know a plan by which Dharmaraja can be subdued and deprived of his kingdom and everything he possesses without shooting an arrow!"

Duryodhana on hearing his uncle's words became very jubilant and asked him:

"What is that plan? Let me hear it now and here."

Sakuni disclosed his plan:

"Duryodhana listen! Dharmaraja is an addict to gambling, especially the play of dice. As a Kshatriya he won't refuse an invitation to play. I am an adept in the game. I will play on your behalf. I will win all the stakes, his kingdom, wealth and everything he possesses... all everything!"

Sakuni and Duryodhana then went to Dhrutharashtra, to get his consent for their plan and urge him to invite Dharmaraja.

Sakuni told Dhrutharashtra:

"O King! Your son Duryodhana is sinking with great anxiety and dejection. You are not taking any care of him!"

Dhrutharashtra loved his son Duryodhana very deeply. He asked him to come near and sit by his side. Caressing him, he asked:

"My son what ails you? What is the reason for your sorrow? You are in possession of all the eight items of wealth. The entire kingdom is at your beck and call. You are enjoying luxurious life like Devendra. You have mastered Vedavedangas, Archery, Gadhayuddha and all Sastras from Krupacharya, Dronacharya and Balarama; all experts in the field. Yet what is wanting? Tell me, my son!"

Duryodhana replied:

"Father, of course I am eating and sleeping like any other person. But, I am bearing insults from all corners."

He then told all about the luxurious life that is being led by the Pandavas and how he was feeling jealous towards them. He further said:

"Father, it is not in the blood of Kshatriyas to be content with what they possess. Fear, compassion and favouritism belittle the status of kings. After seeing the Pandavas' wealth, power, prosperity and popularity, my wealth, power, prosperity and popularity are very insignificant!"

Dhrutharashtra consoled his son:

"Duryodhana, you are my favourite son. Also you are the successor to the throne. Don't cultivate enmity with the Pandavas. Enmity breeds sorrow and destruction. Why are you so hostile towards the Pandavas. Dharmaraja is innocent of what deceit is. His wealth and prosperity is ours also. His friends are our friends also. He does not entertain any jealousy and enmity towards any person. You are equal to him in strength. Son, don't nourish jealousy and enmity! They ruin any person."

Duryodhana did not relish the words of advice of his father. He rebuked him:

"Father, education and worldly knowledge which are of no practical application are useless. Just as the gadget that mixes the food does not know the taste of the food it mixes, you are not conversant with the spirit of the moral science though you have read a lot of it. Patience and contentment are good for a common man but not for a Kshatriya. 'Be after victory' should be the Kshatriya's motto in life. It does not matter if one wins by honest means or dishonest means. The end should be the criterion for any action and not the means."

Sakuni supported Duryodhana saying:

"To defeat Dharmaraja without a war, the only means is by playing dice with him and defeating him in the game and ourselves acquiring all the stakes!"

"Father" continued Duryodhana, "Hypocrisy and deceit should also be in the hands of Kshatriyas in addition to bows and arrows and other armaments and a powerful army to win wars or achieve set purposes. A friend or an enemy is not identified by the birth or caste. Through whomsoever one suffers, he is the enemy. May be, he is a brother or any other relative, it does not matter. A king who keeps mum fully knowing the enemy's advancement in any field, gets ruined. He should put a halt to his enemy's advancement by any means – fair or foul! Pests which destroy the root if allowed untouched they destroy the entire tree also! So, father you just invite Dharmaraja to the play of dice. The rest Sakuni uncle will look after. He will see that all the wealth of Pandavas is won over by us."

Dhrutharashtra said that he would consult Vidura but Duryodhana dissuaded his father from doing so, as he knew that Vidura would advice against the proposal.

Ultimately Dhrutharashtra yielded to the persistent persuasion of his son agreed to invite Dharmaraja to come and play the dice game.

He sent Vidura to go to Indraprastha and invite Dharmaraja, his brothers and other members of his family also on the pretext of inviting them to see the newly constructed Sports Stadium.

Vidura went to Indraprasthanagar and met Dharmaraja. Dharmaraja after formal exchange of courtesies about the welfare of all the relatives on either side, enquired about the purpose of his visit. Vidura said:

"Dharmanandana, I am deputed by the King Dhrutharashtra to invite you all to come and see the beautiful Sports Stadium he has constructed and spend some time playing the game of dice."

"Gambling leads to conflicts. Wise people don't take part in gambling. What is your opinion?" asked Dharmaraja. Vidura replied:

"No body can dispute the opinion that playing dice leads to undesirable evil consequences. I tried to give up this proposal. But the king Dhrutharashtra under pressure from his son Duryodhana and Sakuni did not relent. He has asked me to come over to you and bring you all. You decide whether to accept the invitation or not."

Dharmaraja decided to accept the invitation for the reasons that if the invitation is refused, Dhrutharashtra might get angry and may lead to a conflict which he wanted to avoid and also as it was improper for a Kshatriya king to refuse an invitation for gambling. He along with his brothers, Draupadi and other relatives went to Hastinapur.

The next day after Dharmaraja and his brothers and Draupadi arrived at Hastinapur, he was invited to the game of dice by Sakuni on behalf of Duryodhana.

Dharmaraja told Sakuni:

"Uncle, it is not good to play dice. No valour is required to win the game of dice. Great sages like Asitha, Devala and others with great worldly wisdom have stated that the game of dice is deceitful and not sport. For Kshatriyas, war is the only proper sport apart from hunting expedition to kill cruel wild animals in the forest. You also know this and yet you are inviting me to play dice!"

Dharmaraja was in a dilemma. Due to addiction his mind was urging him to play. On the other hand wisdom urged him to detest from playing.

Sakuni studying the mind of Dharmaraja urged him to play by his cunning arguments.

"There is no deceit... no war in this game! Don't people take part in literary contests? The more learned win over the less learned. What deceit is there in it? In a war also an adept defeats a weak person. What deceit is there in it again? In the game of dice also, it is just the same. If you are afraid of being defeated don't play but don't detest it on moral grounds!"

Dharmaraja's urge to play overtook his dilemma.

"All right... let us play. Who will play with me?" enquired Dharmaraja.

"The money and all the stakes I offer. Sakuni uncle will play on my behalf," said Duryodhana.

The game commenced.

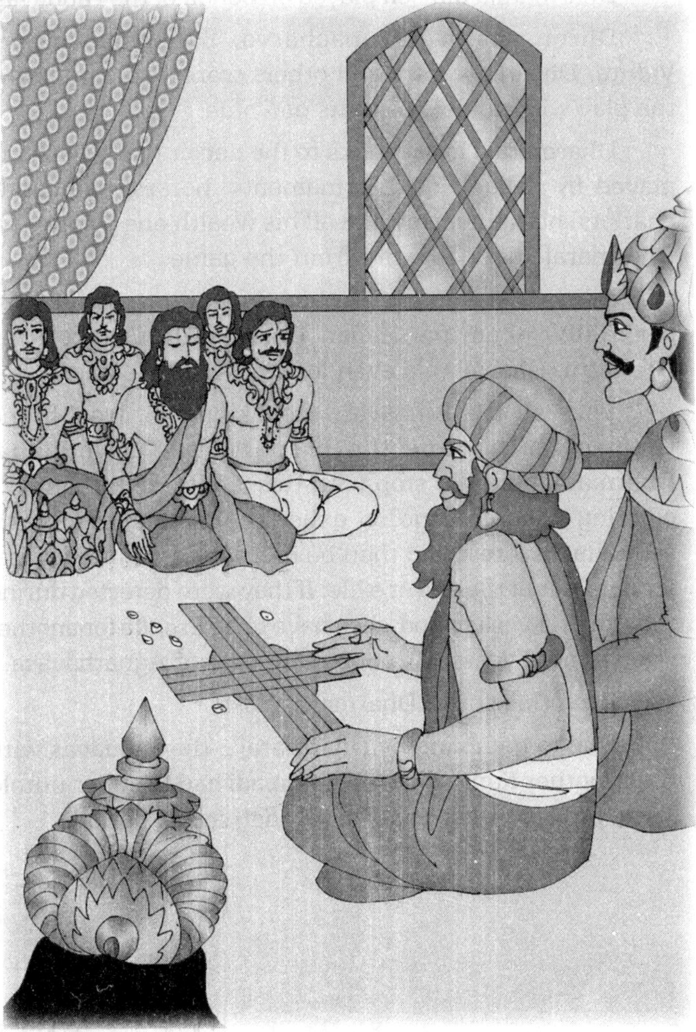

Dharmaraja himself played on behalf of the Pandavas.

Dhronacharya, Krupacharya, Bheeshmacharya, Vidura, Dhrutharashtra and others were also witnessing the play with anxiety as to its outcome.

Dharmaraja lost, thanks to the deceit that was being played by Sakuni, gold, armaments, horses, elephants, chariots, his staff, army and all his wealth one by one. Yet Dharmaraja did not retire from the game.

He then staked his brothers, one after one and lost them all! Sakuni persuaded Dharmaraja to take even Draupadi. Dharmaraja even lost this crucial stake.

Thus all the Pandavas, their kingdom, wealth and themselves became the property of Duryodhana. Dharmaraja did not stop with this. He staked, thanks to cunning Sakuni, to go on exile, all of them, for twelve years into a forest and then be in disguise (Agnathavasa) for one year at the end of exile. If they were detected during the Agnathavasa period, they have to be in exile for another twelve more years with one more year of Agnathavasa.

Even this stake, Dharmaraja lost!

Due to gambling by Dharmaraja, the Pandavas with their mother Kunti and wife Draupadi had to suffer untold misery during their exile and Agnathavasa period.

3. Jealousy

This episode from Mahabharata tells us how, however learned, enlightened and great a person might be, sometimes he falls a victim to jealously and as a consequence gets humiliated. Bruhaspathi, the chief priest of Devatas who was highly learned in Vedavedangas was one such person.

Bruhaspathi had a brother by name Sampartha. He was also equally learned as his brother and also gentle and amenable. On account of this Bruhaspathi felt jealous of his own brother. People do not allow a good person to be as such. Because they are not good persons, they feel jealous of virtuous persons: 'Why should they be good persons,' they feel. Bruhaspathi used to create for his brother all sorts of trouble. Unable to face the troubles from his brother, Sampartha used to spend his life roaming in the town pretending like a mad person.

One Marutha belonging to Ikshaku dynasty acquired huge quantity of gold as a result of a boon he got from Lord Shiva after performing penance. With this gold, he decided to perform a great Yaga. To conduct this Yaga, he decided to invite Bruhaspathi. Apprehending that as a result of the Yaga, Marutha would get more power than Devathas for whom he was a Guru, he declined the invitation. Determined to perform the Yaga, Marutha invited Sampartha. He agreed. On account of this, Bruhaspathi's jealousy against his brother intensified. Worried about this, Bruhaspathi began to lose health and get debilitated.

Devendra, the king of Devathas came to know about the condition of Bruhaspathi and came to see him and asked:

"Oh Guru! why are you getting debilitated day by day. What is standing in the way of your welfare? Are your servants showing any insubordination? Are they not looking after your comforts? Please tell me."

Bruhaspathi replied thus:

"I am being provided with all the comforts. There is no wanting in the service being rendered by the servants. They are showing due respect to me. But..."

Thereafter he could not proceed further, overcome by sorrow.

Devendra pressed Bruhaspathi to reveal the cause of his grief. He then relented and said:

"The King Marutha is performing a great Yaga and my brother who is my enemy is presiding over the Yaga performance. Grief has therefore struck me. As a result I have become like this."

Devendra was surprised on hearing this. He told Bruhaspathi:

"Oh great brahmin! You are getting all your wishes fulfilled. You have acquired great fame as the Priest and Adviser to the Devathas. What evil are you expecting from your brother? Why are you unnecessarily feeling jealous of your brother and getting yourself debilitated?"

Bruhaspathi could not swallow the arrogance of Devendra teaching him. He reminded Devendra about several occasions in the past when he became jealous and wanted to take revenge. He then asked him:

"Would you keep quiet seeing your enemy prospering? I am also no exception. Anyhow you must see the downfall of my brother. He should be withdrawn from the Yaga."

Devendra called for Agnideva and told him:

"You go and see that Sampartha is withdrawn from the Yaga that is being performed by the king Marutha."

Agnideva agreed. On his way he created terror by consuming with his fire everything that came in his way. He met Marutha. Marutha felt very happy that Agnideva himself had come to him. He treated him with great respect and attended to all his needs. Agnideva asked the king:

"Oh King! you must withdraw Sampartha from the Yaga you are performing. I will get Brihaspathi in his place. This is the wish of Devendra."

Sampartha heard these words. He got hurt. He was observing Brahmacharya and had thereby acquired great powers. He warned Agnideva:

"Stop telling such things! If I get angry I can burn you to ashes. Be careful."

Agnideva was aware of the great powers possessed by a person observing Brahmacharya. With those powers one can burn anything into ash. So, he without any further talk returned to Devendra and informed him about all that transpired.

Devendra did not listen to what Agnideva told him. He asked:

"Agnideva, how can anybody burn you to ashes when you can yourself burn everything into ash?"

"Devendra, you are not aware of the power of Brahmacharya," so saying Agnideva reminded him how he was once before got humiliated by the power of a brahmin who practised Brahmacharya.

Devendra then sent a Gandhara to Marutha to tell him to withdraw Sampartha from the Yaga or face his wrath.

The Gandharva went to the king Marutha and gave the message from Devendra. The king did not relent and told the Gandharva:

"It is a sin to betray a friend. I cannot withdraw Sampartha, whatever may be the consequences."

Devendra, angered on hearing the response from the king Marutha, came with his Vajrayudha to subdue the king Marutha. Marutha fearing that Devendra himself was coming with deadly weapon sought shelter under Sampartha.

Sampartha with the power of Penance and Brahmacharya subdued Devendra who then realised the power of Brahmacharya. He then surrendered before Sampartha and begged to be pardoned. He also took the share of offerings due to him from the Yaga as offered by the king Marutha, blessed him and returned to his Kingdom Devaloka. Bruhaspathi then realised that jealousy would bring nothing but humiliation to any person however learned and great one may be.

4. From Sovereign to Servant

This episode from Mahabharata tells us how even great persons have to suffer ignominy of having to serve as servants under persons whom they once ruled. Also the great sage Dowmya gives some pieces of advice as to how a servant under a king should behave and observe certain manners.

Pandavas had to spend in exile from twelve years and then in disguise (Agnathavasa) for one more year on account of an agreement entered into with Duryodhana after their defeat in the game of dice. The exile was nearing completion. Dharmaraja, the eldest of the Pandavas told the sages and the brahmins with whom they had spent the twelve years of exile:

"Sages and brahmins! We are about to complete the twelve years of exile. We have now to spend one year in Agnathavasa. We are all feeling sorrowful for having to leave you all. We don't know where to go and how we have to spend the period of disguise without being detected and identified by anybody."

Dhowmya, one of the sages in the hermitage consoled Dharmaraja saying:

"Dharmaputra! A wise person like you should not feel worried about your Agnathavasa period. Be courageous. Plan your future action. There are instances in the past where even Gods and Devatas were forced to spend some period in disguise to achieve some purpose.

Devendra had to spend some time disguised as a brahmin in Nishada kingdom having been defeated by the demons. But later on he came out, defeated the demons and got back his Indraloka to himself. Even Lord Sri Mahavishnu had to be born as a human being as the son of the Sage Adhithi, as Vamana to teach a lesson to Bali Chakravarthi who was puffed with pride. Lord Srimanarayana entered into the armament of Devendra to kill Vrutrasena, the demon. Lord Sri Mahavishnu again took birth as the son of the king Dasaratha of Ayodhya, underwent untold misery, to kill Ravanasura, the demon king of Lankapuri. Thus, there are several such instances. Yours is also one such instance. So be courageous!"

Dharmaraja and his brothers along with Draupadi then left the place and disappeared into the forest. They then assembled at a place to chalk out the future plan of action. Dharmaraja began consultations first with Arjuna:

"Brave brother Arjuna! You are the most experienced and well-informed about the places. Suggest a suitable place to spend our Agnathavasa."

Arjuna replied:

"You have secured a boon from Yamadhrmaraja ensuring secrecy about our Agnathavasa during the next twelve months. Let us all stay at one place during this period. We have several places to choose from. The kings of Panchala, Matsya, Kalinga and Magadha are all our friends and well-wishers. Yet in my opinion the Kingdom of Matsya ruled by the King Virata is the best place. Viratanagar is a beautiful city and is full of wealth."

Dharmaraja agreed with the suggestion of Arjuna and said:

The king Virata of Matsya kingdom is a very courageous person. He is a good friend of us. He adheres to Dharma at any cost. He is a matured senior oldman. He is not afraid of Duryodhana. So, I fully agree with Arjuna's suggestion. Let us all go there."

Arjuna's eyes were filled with tears. Dharmaraja who performed Aswamedha Yaga and subdued all the kings in the country and who is king of kings has to work as a servant under some king now. These thoughts brought the tears to Arjuna.

Each one of them was then asked to state the disguise under which they would serve the king Virata.

Dharmaraja spoke first:

"I choose to work as an official in the court of the king. I can be giving him advice whenever sought for. I can entertain the king by playing dice with him. I will assume the name of Kankabhat. I can be discussing Astrology, Vedavedantha and moral science with the king as he is interested in them. I will tell him that I worked under Dharmaraja earlier. I will take care to keep up my disguise a secret."

Dharmaraja then turned towards Bheemasena:

"Brother brave Bheemasena! What job do you propose to seek under the king? You are the person who fought with yakshas and demons and killed many of them. You are the person who killed the great demons like Bakasura and Hidambasura. Your Gadha always itches for a fight. Your weakness is anger and emotional outburst. You have to keep them under control lest your identity is exposed."

Bheemasena said:

"I am fully aware of my limitations during the period of Agnathavasa. I am Nala, a cook in the Kitchen of the palace of the king. You know my capacity to cook delicious items of several foods. I am confident of getting praises from the king and his family members. I can also tell the king that I am an experienced wrestler and can beat persons in that field. I can get all the firewood required for the kitchen from the forest myself. I assure you again that I will not do anything that would expose our identity."

It was then Arjuna's turn. Dharmaraja asked him:

"Brave brother, possessor of Gandeeva bow! What are your plans. Let us know."

Arjuna revealed his plan thus:

"I will wear a saree and blouse and enter the apartment of the Queen as Bruhanala and serve the women fold there. You remember I was cursed to become an eunuch by the divine dancer in Indraloka when I visited that place. Urvasi made love to me and I refused the overtures on the ground that she is related to me as a mother! But yet she cursed me. On the intervention of Devendra the curse was modified enabling me to choose the operation of the curse at a time I choose and also that the curse shall operate for one year only. This curse has now come in handy as a boon!

I will decorate myself with bangles made out of wild conches. Heave my hair-style modelled as that of a women. I can teach dance and music to the ladies there. I will tell that I worked under Draupadi before!" So saying he looked at Draupadi and smiled.

On hearing the words of Arjuna, Dharmaraja could not but shed tears saying:

"Oh great warrior Arjuna! What an evil fate has overtaken you. You who is considered to be as great a warrior as Lord Vasudeva Himself, has now to be described as an eunuch and serve ladies and teaches dances!"

Nakula and Sahadeva were then asked to tell their roles under the king Virata.

Nakula said:

"I with the name Damagrandhi will choose to work in the horses stable of the king. You know I am an expert in horse science and also veterinary science. I can also be good charioteer. I will say that I worked before in this capacity under the Pandavas."

Turning to Sahadeva, Dharmaraja said:

"You are equal to Bruhaspathi in intelligence. You beat Sukracharya in Moral science. And in diplomacy there is none equal to you. What job have you chosen under the king?"

Sahadeva replied:

"As my brother looks after horses, I will look after cows. My name will be Tantripala. I will protect the cows from attacks by tiger and other wild animals in the forest while grazing."

Draupadi's turn came. Dharmaraja said:

"You are accustomed to live a life of a princess. How can you be a servant to somebody?"

Draupadi said:

"Don't feel sorrowful about me. I will gladly work as a servant in the queen's apartment. I will be servant-maid to the queen. I will take care of my dignity and purity. I will be Sairandri. I will say that I worked under Draupadi."

Daowmya heard their plans when they came back and told him.

The sage then told Dharmaraja and the others:

"Pandava brothers and Draupadi, listen to a piece of my advice as all of you are hereafter working under the king.

Those who choose to work in Royal palace and courts must be very careful and observe certain manners of good and tactful behaviour.

You should perform your job after assessing the king's mind.

Give advice only when asked for by the king.

Unless sent for don't go to the king.

Shower praises on the king occasionally only.

Obtain king's consent to perform even trivial things.

The king is a fire in human form. So, never go very near him.

Be prompt in executing the orders of the king.

Never be sure of the favour of a King. They change their views and mind frequently.

Even when you are very close to the king, never get into a seat, or his conveyance or his chariot before the king takes his seat. Similarly, get down before the king gets down.

A lazy servant always runs the risk of losing his job.

Never exhibit your joy or sorrow when you are favoured or disfavoured by the king.

Guard the secrets carefully.

Never accept any gifts or rewards from the public.

Don't feel jealous of other servants.

Be very careful about your behaviour with the ladies in the palace. Never try to seek their friendship."

Dharmaraja, his brothers and Draupadi expressed their grateful thanks to the sage for his advice and promised to follow them strictly.

They all then went to the king Virata and managed to join his services as planned.

5. Yudhishtira and the Yakshadevata Quiz

This episode from Mahabharata gives us a number of wise illuminatory facts. Pandavas were about to complete their twelve years sojourn in the forest.

One day a deer came and took away the Arani wood pieces which were used to kindle sacred fire from the hut of a poor brahmin. Without those wood pieces the brahmin would not be able to kindle the sacred fire and perform the daily ritual of Agnihotra. So, he went to the Pandavas who were residing nearby and requested them to recover those wood pieces from the deer.

The Pandava five brothers, Yudhishtira, Bheemasena, Arjuna, Nakula and Sahadeva went to catch the deer. The deer took them to a far off place in the forest and disappeared. As tired they took shelter under a tree to take rest.

All of them were very tired and thirsty. Yudhishtira asked Nakula:

"Brother, get me some water. I am very thirsty. Get to the top of the tree and see if there is any source of water around here."

Nakula climbed to the top of the tree and surveyed around. He came down and told:

"Brother, there appears to be a small tank at not a far off place. Cranes are there. I will go and get you the water."

So saying Nakula went to fetch water. After a long walk he came to a place where there was a small tank. He felt very glad. He took a big leaf from a nearby tree and went to the tank. When he was about to take the water, he heard a voice from the sky.

"Don't touch the water. The tank belongs to me. Without my permission nobody shall be dare enough to touch the water in the tank. Before you touch the water, you have to answer the questions I put!"

But, Nakula did not care the warning. He took and drank water from the tank as he was very thirsty. He came out of the tank and there he immediately felt giddy and fell down unconsciously.

As Nakula did not return even after a long time, Yudhishtira asked Sahadeva to go and find out what had happened to Nakula. Sahadeva went to the tank and found his brother lying unconscious on the ground. He thought that somebody had killed his brother. As he was very thirsty he got into the tank and drank the water. As his brother he was also forbidden to touch the water before he answered the questions put by the strange voice from the sky. Like Nakula he also ignored the warning, drank the water and fell down unconsciously as soon as he came out of the tank.

Then Arjuna was sent to find out why the two brothers did not return. He went to the tank and saw his two brothers lying on the ground unconscious. He was also feeling very thirsty. He went into the tank and was about to take water to drink. He also heard the unidentified voice telling him not to touch the water before answering his questions.

Arjuna angered and shouted:

"Who are you? Come and stand before me. I will see the end of you with my arrow!"

So saying he let the arrow in the direction from which he heard the voice.

"I am Asareeravani! I have no body. So, your arrows cannot harm me. First you answer my questions and then drink the water. Otherwise you will suffer the same fate as your brothers."

But, Arjuna was very thirsty. So, he went and drank the water ignoring the warning like his brothers and he too suffered the same fate as his brothers.

Worried that his three brothers did not return, Yudhishtira sent Bheemasena to find out the reasons for his brothers not returning with water.

Bheemasena too, like all his brothers, ignored the warning of the voice, drank water and fell down unconscious on the ground as soon as he came out of the tank.

Yudhishtira when he saw all his four brothers not returning, he himself went. There he saw all his four brothers lying unconscious on the ground. He thought:

"It appears to be the doing of a Maya. There is not even a slight injury on the bodies. They are not dead as their faces are bright and they are all breathing. There is no indication of any of our enemies having come as there are no footprints of any human being except those of my brothers. May be this is a mischief played by Duryodhana!"

Thus thinking he got into the tank to quench his thirst. Asareeravani again repeated what it said to the four Pandava brothers and warned:

"Your brothers ignoring my warning invited this fate. You are wise. Please answer my questions."

Yudhishtira realised that it was some Yaksha that was speaking. He said:

"Ask the questions. I shall answer to the best of my knowledge."

The question and answer session went on like this:

Question : What is it that makes the Sun rise every morning?

Answer : Brahmam.

Question : Which is it that always be a helping hand?

Answer : Courage.

Question : By studying which Sastra would a man become wise?

Answer : Not by studying any Sastras but by following the footsteps of elderly wise.

Question : Which is more great than the Earth?

Answer : A mother who bears a child!

Question : Which is more sacred than the Sky?

Answer : Father.

Question : Which is faster than Air?

Answer : Mind.

Question : Which is worst than dry straw?

Answer : Worry.

Question : What is required for a traveller?

Answer : Money.

Question : Who is the companion in a home?
Answer : Wife!
Question : Who is the friend of a person nearing the age of death?
Answer : Philanthropy!
Question : What is greatest vessel?
Answer : Earth which contains everything.
Question : What is happiness?
Answer : Good behaviour.
Question : What is to be given up to get the patronage from all?
Answer : Pride. Leave it, everybody likes you.
Question : What is to be given up to get rid of sorrow?
Answer : Anger.
Question : What is to be given up to acquire wealth?
Answer : Desire.
Question : Does Brahmanism comes from Caste, Character or Education?
Answer : Brahmanism does not come either from Caste or from education of Sastras. It comes from good character, and conduct. However educated one is, however learned one is of Sastras, however powerful one is, one does not become a true Brahmin. If one is of a bad character, he will not be entitled to

be called a Brahmin and is equal only to a low-caste person.

Question : What is the most surprising thing in this world?

Answer : Knowing that Death is inevitable, yet everybody is aspiring to live eternally!

Question : This is my last question. I am pleased with your wise answers to all my questions. Only one of your brothers can come out alive. Among your brothers whom do you choose? Tell me. I will give life to him!

Without hesitation Yudhishtira replied: "Nakula!"

"Leaving Bheemasena who has the strength of ten thousand elephants, why did you choose Nakula? It is again Arjuna's strength that is the greatest protection. Yet why did you choose Nakula?" Yaksha asked.

"Oh Yaksha! It is Dharma that protects everybody; neither Bheemasena nor Arjuna. If you neglect Dharma, the same perishes man. My father had two wives, Kuntidevi and Maadridevi. I am the son of Kuntidevi and I am alive. So, the son of Maadridevi, Nakula should be alive. I should not be selfish! It is Dharma!" Yudhishtira answered.

Yaksha said further:

"Oh, my son, all your brothers shall regain life without discrimination. This boon I confer on you."

The person who came in the guise of a deer and Yaksha was no other than Dharmadevata, the father of

Yudhishtira. He had come personally to test the character of his son and he felt extremely happy.

He told Yudhishtira:

"My son, there are only a few days left for your exile to be over. Your one year Agnathavasa (exile in disguise) will also be successfully completed. Your enemies will never be able to identify any of you during that period. This boon also I am conferring on you!"

So saying Dharmadevata disappeared.

6. The Mouse Girl

Once upon a time there was a small little girl mouse in a forest. She used to move about in the forest freely. One day she saw a great sage sitting under a tree with closed eyes in deep meditation. The little mouse gazed at the sage in fascination. Devotion filled in her tiny mind. From that day onwards, the little mouse took on for herself the duty of serving the sage. With her tiny tail she would sweep the ground on which the sage would sit for meditation, sprinkle water over the place with her tiny mouth, bring flowers and fruits from the trees. The sage noticed the loving services of the tiny mouse and loved her very much.

One day as the little mouse went into the depths of the forest to bring fruits and flowers, a huge cat suddenly jumped from above the tree to pounce upon the mouse and eat her up. The mouse was terrified. Somehow she quickly ran aside and entered into a rat hole and saved herself. Till long after that she sat in the rat hole shivering and trembling out of fright. After a few hours she became normal and come to the sage. The sage was surprised at her absence from the morning and when he knew the reason, he pitied the mouse very much. By his power he converted the mouse into a young girl in human form, so that in future she need not be afraid of cats and dogs. The mouse girl was very very happy and continued to serve the sage with great love and respect.

As years passed, the mouse girl grew up into a beautiful young lady. It was the proper time for marriage.

The sage thought that he would find a suitable mouse boy for her and perform her marriage with him. But, the mouse girl did not like it. She said: "Oh my Guru, I am now a human girl. How can I marry a mouse boy? Please allow me to marry the best one."

The sage smiled and said:

"All right, you choose the best bridegroom yourself. I shall give him to you surely."

That day onwards the mouse girl was on the look out for the best of bridegrooms. As she always lived in the forest, she had no occasion to meet any men at all except the great sage. So, she did not know what best people are like. One day as she was collecting fruits and flowers in the forest, she saw a wood cutter felling the trees with an axe. When she saw how the huge tree was cut by him she thought: "Here is my best man." Still she wanted to make sure that he was the best. She watched him for a long time as he was cutting the trees and bundling up the firewood. When he put the firewood on his head and started going into the town, she followed him.

The wood cutter went straight to the house of a rich merchant. He entered the house through the backyard, put the firewood there and came to the merchant who was sitting in the main hall in the house. He saluted the merchant and submitted respectfully.

"Sir! I supplied firewood for you. Please give me the money."

He received the payment and went away.

When the mouse girl saw this, she felt that the wood cutter was only a small fry and that the merchant was far superior to him. So, she dropped all the thought of marrying the wood cutter and kept her watch on the merchant to see if he was the best of all. After sometime, the merchant finished his work at the desk and got out of the house. There a bullock cart was waiting for him. He got into it and the cart started moving. The girl walked very fast behind the cart. The cart after sometime reached the king's palace. There the cart stopped and the merchant got down and went in. The mouse girl followed him.

The king was in durbar. He sat upon the throne dressed in royal robes while all others who were coming were doing obeisance to him and submitting memoranda. The merchant who was having a confident nonchalant air till that moment became very humble once he was in the court. He made a deep obeisance to the king and stood in one corner to await the pleasure of the king.

When the mouse girl saw it, she knew that the merchant was not the best. She dropped all ideas of his becoming the possible bridegroom. She looked and looked at the king who appeared to be the best of all. But, she wanted to check up before she made up her mind to marry him. She too stood in a corner until the durbar was over. The king rose and all arose. The king came out and sat in the palanquin. The bearers lifted it up and started walking. The mouse girl followed.

On the way, whoever saw the king, stopped and made obeisances. The girl's heart swelled up with pride at the greatness of her prospective bridegroom. Suddenly the palanquin stopped. The mouse girl also stopped. The king got out of the palanquin walked forward and prostrated to a sanyasin who was walking on the road. The king touched with great reverence the feet of the sanyasin who blessed the king.

"Surely the sanyasin is greater than the king!" thought the mouse girl. She was happy that she did not make a hurried decision to marry the king. Because here was one who was better still.

Now the girl was in a confused state of mind. She should not jump to conclusions until she met the best. Now she forgot all about the king and followed the sanyasin. All those who met him on the way stopped and bowed to him with great reverence. The girl was very happy to note all this.

By that time they reached a Shiva temple. The sanyasin went in. Needless to say that the mouse girl also followed. The sanyasin went near the Idol (Linga) of Shiva, poured water over the Linga with great respect and prostrated to the Linga and sang verses in his praise.

The girl was surprised.

"Hey, so the Linga is far superior to the sanyasin!" she thought. "Then why should I ever think of the sanyasin? Let me see whether any one else is greater than the Shiva Linga." She waited in the temple whole day. All came in to prostrate and pray, but the Linga remained the same. No one appeared to be greater. At last the night came and all devotees went away. Only the Linga and the mouse girl remained. In the silence of the night, came out a tiny mouse boy dancing and singing. He danced all over the place without any one to hinder him. He went even into sanctum

SURA'S ● Supreme Sacrifice and Other Moral Tales from Mahabharata

sanctorum and continued his dance there. Suddenly he took into his head to jump over the Linga and dance over the head. Up jumped the mouse boy onto the top of the Linga.

44

The Linga did not do anything at all but allowed the mouse boy to do as he pleased.

The mouse girl looked on in amazement. So, the Linga also was not the best. What a cute mouse boy! He was surely the best. He was her proper bridegroom."

The quest of the mouse girl was over. She went back to the sage and prostrated. The sage looked at the girl kindly and asked:

"Have you discovered the best of bridegrooms?"

The mouse girl bent her head shyly and nodded. She whispered:

"Oh, my Guru. The mouse boy in the temple is the best of all. Please make him my husband."

The sage smiled. He knew that the mouse girl would select only a mouse boy!

7. Sarmistha

This episode tells the tale of a daughter who agreed to sacrifice her liberty for life for the sake of her father. Sukracharya was the Guru (teacher) of the demon king Vrishaparva. Devayani was the loving daughter of Sukracharya. Princess Sarmistha was the daughter of Vrishaparva. They were bosom friends.

One day Devayani and Sarmistha went for a picnic in the forest. They went to bathe in a lake, leaving their garments on the bank. The garments got mixed up into a heap due to a severe gale that blew over. Princess Sarmistha came out of the lake after the swim and inadvertently clothed herself in the garments of Devayani. Devayani came out and noticed the mix up. She blamed Sarmistha for appropriating her garments. They began to exchange abuses.

"You must know my father is supreme head of the State!" boasted Sarmistha.

"What does it matter? My father is the preceptor of all the Asuras, including your father, and he must prostrate before my father."

"Your father, you must remember, is living on the bounty of the king, my father."

The quarrel developed to such a fierce stage that Asura maidens of Sarmistha threw Devayani into a dry well nearby and went away leaving her alone.

She remained in the well sobbing unable to come out. Just then the emperor Yayati of Puru race happened to go that way during his hunting expedition. He heard the sobbing cries of Devayani. He came and peeped into the well. Yayati rescued her by lifting her from the well holding her hands. The emperor Yayati and Devayani introduced themselves to each other. Devayani decided not to enter the capital of the kingdom of Vrishaparva.

Devayani fell in love with Yayati and told him:

"Oh Emperor! You have held my right hand. It means you have taken me as your wife according to dharma-sutra. I consider you worthy to be my husband."

Yayati however said:

"I am a Kshatriya and you are a brahmin girl. You are also the daughter of Sukracharya, the renowned teacher of Asuras. You must therefore obtain the consent of your father."

So saying he went away.

Sukracharya having come to know the sad events and the determination of his daughter not to come to the capital city, himself came to her daughter who was squatting under a tree near the well and tried to console her and persuade her to come to the capital city.

"A worthy person should control his anger and emotional outburst. Scriptures say that he who sheds anger is superior to the person who performs a hundred yagas. The wise will ignore childish pranks and prattle."

Devayani was not in a mind to listen to any moral or ethic discourse. She told her father how arrogant was Sarmistha and roused the pride of Sukracharya by questioning him:

"Are you a minstrel extolling the glories of the king? Are you a parasite, existing on the benevolent grace of the king?"

SURA'S ● Supreme Sacrifice and Other Moral Tales from Mahabharata

She began to weep bitterly. He was moved by his wounded pride. He vowed to teach a lesson to Sarmistha for her insolent and arrogant action.

Devayani felt very happy.

Sukracharya lost no time in going straight to Vrishaparva and told him:

"O King! I cannot serve you any longer. I put up with all the affronts of your attendants, when they killed Kacha many a time though he was a pious pupil who served me with dedication and was never guilty of any sin. Now your daughter has insulted and hurt my daughter, Devayani. I am going out of your kingdom as my daughter refuses to stay any more in your kingdom."

Vrishaparva was taken aback and could not afford to be without Sukracharya.

Vrishaparva went to Devayani with all his retinue and implored her pardon. Devayani however put a condition to pardon him:

"The arrogant Sarmistha should be made over to me as a slave-maid for life and attend on her in the house into which she would be given in marriage."

Sarmistha when told by her father of the demand of Devayani was magnanimous enough to sacrifice her liberty for life for the sake of her father. She said:

"My father shall not lose the venerable preceptor due to my hasty emotional act."

Her sacrifice was hailed as a noblest act.

Later on Devayani married Yayati.

Sarmistha followed Devayani to the palace of Yayati along with her, as her maid-in-waiting.

One day Sarmistha and Yayati happened to meet in the garden alone. She then revealed her royal lineage to the emperor. Yayati had already heard the unique sacrifice she had made for the sake of her father. Yayati was impressed by her external beauty and internal beauty of character.

She was the great daughter of a little king while Devayani was a little daughter of a great master.

Yayati married Sarmistha secretly. She begot two sons.

Devayani came to know about the secret marriage of her husband with Sarmistha and the two sons born to them. She was enraged. She reported this to her father Sukracharya who cursed Yayati with premature old age. This affected the marital relation of Devayani also. This was not what she expected.

Devayani and Yayati requested Sukracharya to repeal the curse. Sukracharya told Yayati.

"I can't repeal the curse. But, I can permit you to exchange the curse with any other who is prepared to transfer his youth to you and take your old age. Yayati requested all his sons one by one to come to his rescue. Yayati even offered to take back his old age after sometime. But, none of the sons expect the last of the five sons, Puru obliged his father.

Yayati regained his youth and enjoyed sensual pleasures in the garden of Kubera in the company of an Apsara maiden. In due course he realised that the urge for sensual pleasure was insatiable. So, he re-exchanged his youth to old age from his son Puru.

He rewarded his son Puru for his loyalty and filial love by bestowing the kingdom to him and disinherited the other sons. He retired to forest to spend the rest of his life in peace and penance.

8. Bhargava Rama

This episode tells the tale of grateful son who did not hesitate to behead his own mother to obey the orders of his father.

Chyavana a sage belonged to Brugurishi dynasty. He was by nature a hardnut to crack. He refused to worship and offer 'havana-homa' to Indra. He refused to yield to the advice of the sages. Indra himself warned him. But, Chyavana was adamant. Indra got angry and cursed Chyavana:

"Let old age overtake you immediately." Everybody thought that once he lost his youth, he would come round. But, Chyavana did not worship Indra.

Divine doctors, Aswinikumara however later restored Chyavana to his youthful age. It is another story by itself.

Indra and Chyavanarishi reconciled with each other. Richika was born in the family of Chyavana. Richika became the Rajaguru (Royal Priest) to the king Mahishmatha. Mahishmatha was the unconquered king of all he surveyed. There was none in equal to Mahishmatha in valour.

The king became conceited and a despot. He even began to be indifferent and disobedient to his guru Richika.

Richika after cursing the king, left the place along with his followers. He went to the king Gadhi, who was ruling the kingdom along the river Saraswati. He belonged to the dynasty of Bharata. This king invited him with all reverence and requested him to stay as his guest.

Later on, the king Gadhi gave his daughter Satyavati to the sage Richika in marriage. They lead a happy married life. A son was born to them. He was Jamadagni. He became the pupil of Maharishi Agastya.

Jamadagni married Renuka, and lived in a hermitage. They had children. Renuka was again pregnant. It was confinement time. Thunders and lightnings blazed across the sky. It looked like a deluge overtaking the world. The ashramites all waited in great anticipation. Jamadagni was immersed in deep prayer and meditation.

The cry of a new born child was heard. A male child. He was named Rama.

His thread marriage was celebrated while he was eight years old.

He took his education under Maharishi Viswamitra.

Rama was engaged in a war in Aryavartha. That day having slaughtered all his enemies, he was taking rest.

Three disciples came running from the Ashram of Jamadagni and stood before Rama. Fear was dancing on their faces. Their bodies were shivering. They were speechless. Eyes were filled with tears.

"What has happened?" asked Rama with anxiety writ on his face.

No reply came.

"Don't hesitate. Speak at once," asked Rama calmly.

"Your two brothers died in the battle," spurted one of them with courage returning to him.

"How is father?" enquired Rama.

Again silence.

"Tell me............no room for fear!"

He is wandering like a mad man along the Saraswati river shores. He is not speaking to anybody!"

"Tell me what is ailing my father? Is not my mother attending on him? Tell me where is my beloved mother?" enquired Rama.

"Mother has deserted the ashram........ is living with a Gandharva king."

Rama's body shivered with fear and eyes reddened with anger.

Rama wore the leather chest armour and took the axe, his armament.

"I am proceeding to the ashram, follow me!"

So saying Rama walked away briskly towards his black horse and jumped on it.

Bhargava Rama's black horse stormed into the Jamadagni ashram.

"Where is my father?" thundered Rama.

"There he is on the banks of the river," meekly said one disciple.

Rama got down from the horse and went towards the river.

His father was there with his head hung in humiliation and shame.

"Father!" shouted Rama.

"Rama... my dear Rama... you have come!" Jamadagni came briskly and embraced his son affectionately. Tears rolled down his eyes.

"Father! What has happened?" exclaimed Rama.

"Rama... your mother, my wife deserted us and eloped with a Gandharva king. Has brought a blackspot on our dynasty itself!" wailed Jamadagni.

"My mother.... the mother of Bhargava Rama.... Renuka Devi looked upon as a mother by one and all.. did such a women elope with a Gandharva king? It can never be true!... it can never be!" asserted Rama emphatically.

"I had relied on you to obey my words. The other children have disobeyed," said Jamadagni.

"I am not so stupid as not to obey my father. Your word is like Veda to me. Tell me. What shall I do to bring joy to you. I am ready to do it!" promised Bhargava Rama.

"Go...... bring your mother here. In the presence of all here behead her!" said Jamadagni.

"I shall obey your command." Bhargava Rama prostrated before the feet of his father, obtained his blessings and went away.

Outskirts of the towering Himalaya mountains where they touch the earth. There a small village. Near the village Bhargava Rama sat under the shade of a tree. His horse was grazing. The villagers mistaking Rama to be soldier came to attack him. But, on learning that he was the son of Renuka Devi, made their obeisance and invited him into their village.

Renuka Devi was residing in a hut in that village. She would return to her hut everyday in the afternoon. He learnt from the villagers that everyday Renuka would go to the hut where the Gandharva king was residing in the morning on that route.

Renuka came out of her hut and started towards the hut of the Gandharva king. People were following her with devotion and respect. Some women were even offering her 'Arati'. Some were taking the dust under her feet and placing it on their heads.

His joy knew no bounds when he saw his mother who looked like a goddess. It came as a surprise to him when he saw her coming from a hut, instead of a palace of Gandharva king as was alleged by his people. But, he had given a word to his father which he had to honour. He controlled his wavering mind, made his heart firm, and decided to carry out his father's command.

Renuka saw her son Rama under the tree. Her heart was filled with joy. She came running towards him to embrace her beloved son crying:

"Rama... my beloved son Rama!"

He told her that his father had sent him there.

"He has sent you to kill me, as he had done earlier by sending your brothers!" she said calmly.

"Yes, I have come to kill you. You are the wife of Maharishi Jamadagni. You are a woman who has come to lead a family life with a new person deserting your husband. You don't deserve to live!" Bhargava Rama had the courage to tell her.

"I have also passed on the same punishment to a woman who had committed the same sin!" she said.

"Then, mother, why did you commit the same sin?" asked Rama.

"Your father is a very wise man, a great sage and 'tapasvi'. I did no injustice to him. But, he did not think over why his wife did like that. My dear son... come... kill me... free me from this mortal frame."

Bhargava Rama became dumb founded.

"Mother... let us go to the ashram... accompany me."

"I am unable to come, my son. In the eyes of all, I am a downfallen woman. I gave four sons to Bhrugu dynasty. Among them courageous, revered one is Bhargava Rama. I was there committed the 'Dharma' that was there. I did not come over to this place to enjoy any luxury. Leaving a husband who is godlike, I did not come here to enjoy bodily pleasure of Gandharva king. I came here only to discharge another 'Dharma' (duty). I had to give up the earlier duty as in my view the present duty is a better one. However, yet, I consider that leaving the duty of serving the husband is a sin and I deserve punishment. Kill me!" Renuka told.

"Mother... I will of course kill you obeying father's command. But, mother, will you enlighten me what sort of duty it was to desert your husband, Jamadagnirishi?" asked Rama.

"Of course, I will. Follow me. The Gandharva will tell you everything."

Rama followed her mother Renuka. A cluster of huts beyond there. People who saw Renuka coming from a distance shouted:

"Oh, mother is coming.... Our goddess is coming!"

Bhargava Rama was bewildered. When he reached them, he saw they were all lepers. Renuka nursed them all, anointed them with pastes, and served them food.

SURA'S ● Supreme Sacrifice and Other Moral Tales from Mahabharata

"Let Renuka mother live a thousand years!" cried the lepers.

Renuka went further. Bhargava followed. They reached a big hut. On a mat the Gandharva king was lying. He was also a leper.

"Mother... welcome to you. We are giving you trouble... Death is delaying taking us!"

Bhargava Rama was stunned. She introduced her son to the king as her beloved son, Rama.

"I have heard his name. He is an incarnation of Lord Vishnu. Very learned and most courageous person. My hands have become inauspicious on account of leprosy to do you even 'namaskar'. Deliver us from this ailment!" pleaded the Gandharva king.

They came out of the hut and proceeded towards the hut of Renuka.

"Kill me son!" Renuka told her son.

"I am born to uphold dharma and not to violate it. You accompany me to our hermitage. Father has forgotten his dharma. I will let him know his dharma and will uphold dharma!" He went out saying:

"I will return in a few moments."

He went to the place where the Gandharva king and other lepers were staying, killed them all and returned.

He then got his mother mount the horse by force and came to his hermitage galloping.

A large number of people had gathered there. He brought his mother and placed her at the feet of his father. Renuka touched her husband's feet in reverence.

His body electrified. He looked at her and commanded:

"Behead her!"

"I will obey thy command. But, one request," asked Bhargava Rama.

"Ask, my loyal son," said Jamadagni.

"After I behead my mother.... thereafter you will not see my body... I mean I will die," announced Rama.

"Are you speaking truth?" asked his father.

"You are a Maharishi. You are aware of everything. Considering that your dharma has been violated by her, you have given orders to behead her. I will obey your orders. You will feel happy."

"But, I feel immense sorrowful. How your dharma is important to me, to kill my mother who gave birth to me and lead a family life of forty years with you, is a violation of dharma for me. For violation dharma, I also deserve punishment like my mother!" said Bhargava Rama and also explained to his father the humanitarian service his mother was rendering to the Gandharva king and the other lepers.

"Bound by the word given to my father I will kill my mother who gave birth to me, and then die to be born again in this same Bhrugu dynasty. Please permit me."

The haze that had covered the mind of Jamadagni melted away and he saw reason. He lifted the kneeling son, embraced him and exclaimed.

"Rama, you are not a human being. You are a God. I did not realise you are the very incarnation of the Lord Vishnu."

"Father let me obey your command," insisted Rama.

Filled with renounce and tears rolling down his cheeks, Jamadagni said:

"Renuka! my wife you are 'pativrata'. Till now you were dead so far I am concerned. It is not proper to kill you again. Come.. propagate our progeny." So saying he consoled her.

Bhargava Rama and others' joy knew no bounds. Everybody shouted cries of joy.

"Victory to Jamadagni!"

There is another version of the same episode:

Hermitage of sage Jamadagni. Most sacred cottage. Jamadagni and Renuka were living in it. A number of disciples were learning Vedas and doing service to their master. The first three sons were all males. Then, Rama was born. His armament was an axe. 'Parasu' means axe. Hence, he got the name Parasurama.

All the children grew up. Parasurama had gone out on some business. Renuka went to fetch water from the river Ganga for her husband's daily worship. From a distance she saw a Gandharva by name Chitraratha sporting in the river waters with some divine dancers.

Renuka gazed at the radiant youthful body of the Gandharva. The sight of some women playing in the river waters with a youth, tempted her mind. The Gandharva's image stayed in her mind. She stood gazing at him for a long time. After the Gandharva and the divine dancers left the river, she regained her senses and returned to the hermitage.

She was feeling guilty of misbehaviour. She came and stood before her husband who questioned.

"Renuka, why late today. Did anything happened there?"

Renuka simply stood with her head bent down and dumb.

Jamadagni through his visionary powers came to know what had happened.

"Shameless woman! Desire on other men!" shouted with rage Jamadagni.

"She does not deserve to be alive!" decided the sage. "But how to kill?"

He called his sons. They came and waited for his father's orders.

"Behead your mother and make me happy!" commanded Jamadagni.

To kill the mother who gave birth to them? The mother who brought them up like a goddess?

They refused.

Parasurama who had gone out, returned just then.

"Rama, my beloved son. You have come. Behead your mother. This is my command. Kill your brothers also who have disobeyed me!" commanded Jamadagni to his loyal son, Parasurama.

Parasurama without hesitation and without asking any questions carried out the command of his father, first by beheading his mother and then his brothers with his axe.

Jamadagni felt very happy. He became calm. His love towards Parasurama increased many fold. He asked him:

"Rama, choose any boon, it shall be given."

"Father what else can I choose except your blessings, my beloved mother and brothers? Give them all life back!" implored his father.

"So it shall be!" so saying Jamadagni sprinkled sacred water sanctified on the bodies of the dead. They all woke up alive.

All of them begged Jamadagni to forgive their faults. Renuka fell on the feet of her husband. Jamadagni consoled her saying:

"It is not your fault. Fate had written that you should have a second life (Punarjanma). Hence, all this happened. Let us go together. It is time for yagna." He lead her taking her hands into his.

This sage Jamadagni is shining as one of the stars of Saptharishi cluster of Stars in the sky, even today.

9. Garuthmantha

This episode describes the sacrifice of Garuthmantha and how he risked his life to get his mother freed from slavery.

Kadruva and Vinatha were the two wives of Kasyapaprajapathi. One day evening Kadruva and Vinatha went on a stroll on the sea shore.

A horse was grazing at a distance.

Kadruva asked, "Can you tell the colour of the horse?"

"Can you not see, it is white," replied Vinatha.

"But its tail is black," said Kadruva.

"No. The tail is also white," asserted Vinatha.

They wanted to go near the horse and verify. As it was getting dark Kadruva suggested that it might be verified the next morning.

They agreed on a bet. Whoever has seen the colour of the tail correct shall be entitled to have the other woman as a servant-maid for life long.

As soon as they returned home, Kadruva called her all serpent children and told them:

"All of you proceed to the sea shore before dawn tomorrow. There you will find a horse. You all entwine the tail of the horse as black hairs."

Her serpent sons refused to be party to such a deceit. She then cursed them:

"Let all of you perish in the fire of the Sarpa Yaga conducted by Janamejaya!"

Hearing the curse, one of her sons, Karkotaka agreed to obey her orders and fulfill her wish.

The next morning, after dawn, Vinatha and Kadruva went to the sea shore and saw the horse's tail. It looked black. So, Kadruva won the bet. Vinatha became Kadruva's servant maid.

Garuthmantha was the son of Vinatha. He was eagle-like in body. Kadruva told him:

"Son you shall also be a servant like your mother. You carry my children on your back, fly and entertain them."

Garuda, as he was called also, agreed to it.

As days passed, Garuda got vexed with this chore of carrying his step-brothers on his back and entertaining them. He asked to tell him the way to get rid of the servitude. They told him:

"Get us Nectar (Amrut) which gives eternal life to those who drink it."

Garuda agreed to get it. He went and asked his mother:

"Mother I have the capacity to secure the Nectar. But, I require a lot of food during my effort to get it. Where do I find it?"

She told him:

"Son, in the midst of the sea, there is a small island, where you can get all the food you require."

He flew unto the sky, journeyed swiftly and reached the island. The food in the island was not sufficient for him. He was still hungry. On the way he met Kasyapa, his father, to tell him the way to get all the food he required. Kasyapa told him:

"There is a lake nearby. Here one elephant and a tortoise are fighting with each other, each trying to kill the other. They were brothers in their former life. Their names were Vibhanu and Supreethi. They were quarrelling over division of their property. They are continuing their quarrelling in this life also after taking birth as an elephant and a tortoise. The elephant looks like a big hillock and the tortoise like a big cloud. They will be sufficient to quench your hunger."

Garuda reached the lake. He took the elephant by one of his nails and the tortoise by another nail of the other leg, and flew into the sky. On the way when he tried to sit on a branch of a big banyan tree, the branch broke away. A sage by name Valakeylyulu was doing penance hanging on the branch with this head down. Garuda to prevent the sage from falling down with the branch took the branch in his beak and took it to safe place where Kasyapa was staying. Valakeylyulu sage blessed Garuda.

Garuda reached Devaloka where Nectar was kept. Devendra came to know from his guru Bhruhaspathi that Garuda had come to take away the Nectar.

Devendra made arrangements by arranging guard around the vessel containing the Nectar. Soldiers with different armaments kept guard around the vessel.

The episode behind the birth of Garuda is as follows:

Once Kasyapaprajapathi performed a yaga to get children born to him. All the sages assisted him in the performance of yaga. Valakeylyulu was one of the persons entrusted with bringing 'Samidha' (Sacred wood) for the yaga. Devendra was bringing a bundle of samidha as big as a hillock while Valakeylyulu was bringing a very tiny bundle proportionate to his tiny body. Devendra laughed and humiliated the sage. The sage retaliated the conceited Devendra by cursing him:

"A bold and strong powerful person who would take the body of a bird will be born to teach you a lesson for your conceit."

Garuda defeated and killed all the soldiers guarding the vessel containing the Nectar.

Yet he was obstructed by big flames surrounding the vessel. He quenched those flames by river waters and reached the vessel. He overcame all the other obstructions finally, took the vessel into his hands and flew up into the sky. Lord Vishnu pleased with the boldness of Garuda asked him to choose a boon.

Garuda with all humility bowed to the Lord Vishnu and said:

"I don't aspire for anything except your immediate shelter eternally. Make me the Emblem of your flag! Give me eternal life devoid of death."

"Not only shall you be the Emblem of my flag but you shall be my Vahana (conveyance) forever!"

Garuda's joy knew no bounds.

Devendra came and attacked Garuda. Even the Vajrayudha could not do anything. Devendra then pleaded with him:

"O Garuda! If you give this Nectar to the serpents, they would obtain eternity and will be a source of immense harm to the world."

"But Devendra, I have undertaken this mission to obtain freedom from bondage to my mother. The moment I hand over this to them, you can snatch it away from them. I will not interfere!"

Devendra agreed. He also reciprocated by conferring a boon to Garuda:

"The serpent community shall form your food hereafter!"

Garuda placed the vessel containing Nectar on a 'Dharba' grass. "You take your bath, come and drink the Nectar. Release my mother from bondage," he said to the serpent community.

They all agreed and went out to take a bath. Devendra came swiftly and took away the vessel. Returning from the bath, not finding the vessel, the serpents licked the surface of the grass on which the vessel had been placed earlier, due to which their tongue split into parts.

Garuthmantha has become a synonym for a loyal and dutiful son.

10. Bhishmacharya

This episode from Mahabharata tell us how a grateful son vowed to be a bachelor throughout his life to fulfill the wishes of his father. The king Prateepa was the most famous king belonging to Puru dynasty. He was an ideal king.

After ruling his country with justice, equity and prosperity, he went to the banks of the sacred river Ganga and commenced performing penance.

One day the river Ganga taking the form of a beautiful young maid came and sat on the right lap of the king and looked at him seriously and seductively.

"Oh lotus-eyed damsel, who are you? Why have you come to me?" asked Prateepa.

"I am Jaahnavi, the daughter of the sage Jhahanu. I wish to have you as my husband!" she told.

The king was surprised but he calmly told her:

"I even don't look at any woman expect my wife. Only a daughter sits on the right lap of a person. I have no objection to take you as my daughter-in-law in due course when my son comes to his youth."

Ganga, satisfied, left the king.

Shantanu, the son of Prateepa in due course blossomed into a beautiful young man. Prateepa crowned him the king and said:

"My son Shantanu, I have promised a young woman who met me on the banks of the river Ganga long back, to take her as my daughter-in-law. When she meets you, accept her as your wife and keep up my promise. In our dynasty we never break promises."

Years passed.

One day, the king Shantanu went on a hunting expedition. After killing several wild animals, he was taking rest on the banks of the river Ganga.

Ganga took the form of an young maid again and appeared before the king Shantanu. The young Shantanu infatuated by the exquisite beauty of the maid before him, fell in love at first sight.

Ganga brought to the notice of the king the promise made to her by his father.

Shantanu without any hesitation said:

"You shall be my wife!"

"But, oh young man! before I accept, you have to agree to certain conditions imposed by me."

The young king was so infatuated by her beauty that he said:

"Surely I will abide by any conditions imposed by you. Let me hear those conditions!" asked the king.

"Then listen to them. You should never question any of my actions. If you, I shall be at liberty to direct and leave you once for all!" said Ganga.

The king agreed and married Ganga Devi. Six sons were born to the king Shantanu. Strangely, as soon as a son was born, Ganga Devi would take the child to the river Ganga and throw it into it. King Shantanu dared not question her action, lest she should leave him once for all, in keeping with her condition at the time of marriage.

SURA'S ● Supreme Sacrifice and Other Moral Tales from Mahabharata

When the seventh son was born and Ganga Devi was about to take the child to the river to throw into it, Shantanu could no longer bear her inhuman action, objected and asked for reason for her behaviours. She replied:

"Oh king! There is an episode behind my action. Due to a curse by the great sage Vasista, the seven devathas called Vasuvoos had to take birth on this earth. I agreed to give birth to them and throw them into the river to give them release from the curse. Thus this seventh child is a chip of those great divine persons. He will shine as the greatest person of your dynasty. I will take him with me. I no longer live with you as you have broken your word and questioned my action. I will keep this boy with me, give him education in all fields, thereafter bring him and hand him over to you!"

So saying Ganga Devi along with the boy left the king Shantanu and disappeared.

Twenty four years passed.

One day while Shantanu was resting on the banks of the river Ganga, Ganga Devi brought an young robust man and after obeisance said:

"Oh king, this is your son whom I am bringing back after educating him in all branches of Sastras and warfare. Take him with you." And then she disappeared.

Being the son of Ganga Devi, he was named Gangeya. Four more years passed.

One evening when the king Shantanu was strolling on the sands of the river Ganga, he saw a young beautiful lotus eyed maid. She was the daughter of the king Nishada. She was carrying passengers in a boat from one bank of the river to the other. The king fell in love with her. He approached her father and requested him to give his daughter Sathyavati in marriage to him.

The king Nishada was too glad to agree to the proposal of the king Shantanu. But, he stipulated a condition that Shantanu should agree and promise to make the son born out of his wedlock to his daughter alone the heir to the throne of the kingdom.

King Shantanu could not agree to the proposal as according to the custom, Gangeya his eldest son was entitled to be crowned as his successor. Apart from this, he loved Gangeya so much that he could hardly even think of doing any injustice to him.

So, the king Shantanu returned to the capital disappointed, dejected and love-sick.

Observing his father's melancholy, Gangeya enquired and ascertained from the minister the cause for his father's sadness.

Gangeya along with the ministers and some elderly courtiers went to Nishada king and assured him:

"Your daughter's son alone shall become the heir to the kingdom and in witness of all the gods, I give up my claim to the kingdom. Please fulfill my father's desire."

But the king Nishada, who was very clever, said:

"Oh youngman, I have full faith in you and your promise but what guarantee is there that your progeny would not claim their right of inheritance?"

Then Gangeya said:

"Oh king Nishada, I vow that I remain a bachelor throughout my life so that there won't be any progeny of mine!"

Nishada was very much pleased and agreed to give his daughter Sathyavati in marriage to the king Shantanu.

Gods from heaven hailed the decision of Gangeya and the thunderbolt-like vow to remain a life long bachelor, just to fulfill the desire of his father, and blessed him.

"Oh great Gangeya, you shall henceforth be called "Bhishma" and your sacrifice shall be written in golden letters in the annals of the great land in which you are born!"

Shantanu also blessed his son and conferred on him a boon.

"My son for the great sacrifice you have made I confer on you the boon to discard this physical body of yours at your will!"

To Sathyavati and Shantanu were born two sons Chitrangada and Vichitraveerya.

After the death of Shantanu, Chitrangada was crowned the king. But, before long Chitrangada died in a battle with a Gandharva.

The king of Kasi had three daughters, Amba, Ambika, and Ambalika.

The king of Kasi had arranged the marriage of his three daughters by Swayamvara. But, Bhishma brought the three brides by force to get them married to Vichithraveerya.

Out of the three daughters, Amba told Bhishma that she had already given her heart to the king Salva and wanted to marry him. Bhishma let her go to Salva and married Ambika and Ambalika to Vichitraveerya and also crowned him the king.

When Amba went to Salva, he rejected her and refused to marry her as she was eloped by Bhishma. Bhishma also refused to marry her to Vichitraveerya.

To take revenge against Bhishma, Amba on the advice of Rajarishi Hothravahana went to Parasurama who was doing penance on the Mahendragiri mountain. She went to Parasurama and told her story. Parasurama said:

"I feel sorry for your plight. I will summon Bhishma responsible for your miserable plight and direct him to prostrate before your feet and give an apology. I don't use the bow and arrow at present as I am under a vow now."

But, Amba insisted on slaying Bhishma, and Parasurama unable to resist her prayer, went to Hastinapura where Bhishma was staying. Bhishma refused to take Amba into his family fold and a battle took place between Bhishma and Parasurama.

In the midst of the battle the sage Narada intervened and stopped the battle between Bhishma and Parasurama.

Sage Narada and elders advised Amba to forget and forgive. But, she did not relent. She performed penance and with a boon from Paramashiva, she took her birth as a female child to the king Drupada. Though a female child, the king Drupada brought her up as a male Sikhandi and well educated her in archery and other faculties.

When she came to marriage age, Drupada married her disguised as a bridegroom to the daughter of the king of Dasarna. The king of Dasarna came to know through his daughter that she has been married to another woman only and Drupada has played a fraud on them.

Sikhandi went into a forest, met a Yaksha who on compassionate ground agreed to transfer his masculine form to her and take her female form. Later on, the king of Yakshas, Kubera came to know about this and became angry at what his servant Yaksha had done. Kubera cursed the Yaksha:

"You shall continue to be a female till Sikhandi dies!"

From thereon Sikhandi was waiting for an opportunity to take revenge on Bhishma.

Mahabharata war began between Kauravas and Pandavas.

On the advice of the Lord Sri Krishna, Pandavas went to Bhishma and implored him to reveal the way to succeed in the great war.

Bhishma told them:

"Children... you are all aware that I don't fight with persons who stand before me without protection and without a bow and arrows with them. Also I don't fight with women. I don't fight with a coward and also one who has a chariot with an inauspicious flag decorating it. You make Sikhandi who is having all these characteristics stand before me in the battle and thus defeat me."

It was the next day of the battle.

Arjuna came to the battlefield with Sikhandi standing before him in the chariot.

Bhishma came and stood opposite to him. Sikhandi was tormenting Bhishma with his sharp arrows but Bhishma was not retaliating with even a single arrow. One of the arrows of Sikhandi broke the bow of Bhishma. Arjuna was also hitting Bhishma from behind Sikhandi with his arrows.

It was about the evening.

Bhishma's body was full of pierced arrows. Before the sunset, Bhishma unable to bear the agony fell on the ground. But, his body did not touch the ground and stood lying down on the bed of arrows piercing his body.

Everybody in the battlefield, both Kauravas and Pandavas was sunk in deep sorrow, came and stood around him respectfully.

Bhishma said to Arjuna and others:

"I do not want to leave this body till this "Dakshinayana" period is over and "Uttarayana" period starts which is auspicious. Till then I would be lying on the bed of these arrows only."

He then turned to Duryodana and said:

"Don't remove these arrows or give me any medical treatment. Cremate me with these arrows."

Uttarayana, when the sun turns his journey towards the north, came.

In the presence of all his relations both Pandavas and Kauravas at the auspicious moment Bhishma looked at the Lord Krishna who was standing by his side. Lord Krishna looked at Bhishmacharya smiling. His Atmajyoti (soul-light) came out of his body and travelled into the eternal universe, illuminating the entire universe. Thus came to an end the illustrious life of one of the greatest men of the Mahabharata epic.

11. Bakasura, the Demon

This episode from Mahabharata tells us how in a family each member was prepared to sacrifice even his or her life for the welfare of others and that it is a duty and moral obligation to help those who helped us.

Pandavas were spending their exile and Agnathavasa (Living in disguise) in a town called Ekachakranagar. They were living disguised as brahmins. They were eking their livelihood by begging in the brahmin's street. The five brothers, Yudhishtira, Bheemasena, Arjuna, Nakula and Sahadeva, were handing over the food they secured by begging to their mother Kuntidevi. She was serving the food among them all. She used to divide the food brought, into two parts. One half was served to Bheemasena and the other half to all the others including herself. Being the son of Vayu Deva, Bheemasena was stronger than the other brothers. His hunger was also manifold of those of the others. The share of food Bheemasena was getting was hardly sufficient for him. He became very lean and this worried his brother Dharmaraja and his mother Kuntidevi.

During their stay at Ekachakranagar, Bheemasena made friendship with a potter. He used to dig and get him the mud required to prepare the pots. The potter in return gave a big pot to Bheemasena. Bheemasena used to carry that big pot to beg food. Children used to play fun whenever they came across Bheemasena with the huge pot and his pot-belly.

One day all except Bheemasena had gone to the town for begging. Bheemasena was staying in the house protecting their mother Kuntidevi. In one of the apartments of the house in which the Pandavas were residing the owner of the house was also residing.

Bheemasena and Kuntidevi heard cries, weeping and wailings from the owner's apartment. Kuntidevi went to their house to find out the cause for their distress.

The head of the family was shouting with tears flowing:

"You all didn't listen to me when I suggested that we should leave this town. I told you several times. You were adamant saying that you don't want to leave the place where we were all born and grew up. You are insisting on staying here even after we lost our parents, all kith and kin. I can't leave you all here and go to a place of safety. You are my life-partner. You are my friend and also my wife who gave a son and helped to perpetuate my progeny. I can't desert you. Neither can I send you as a prey to the cruel demon Bakasura. As you all know today is our turn to send one member of our family to that wicked demon Bakasura, I can't send you as I told you just now. Over our daughter we have no right. She has to be got married and sent to her husband to lead her own life. It is our duty to do so. It is our duty to protect her till she is married away. It is Adharma and a sin to sacrifice our young son as he has to perpetuate our progeny as you have done. You didn't listen to me earlier. Now today we have to suffer this agony as a result of your adamant attitude all these days. I myself can't go to the demon as who will look after all of you in my absence. So better let all of us go to demon and die in his hands or commit suicide together!"

The wife of the brahmin retorted:

"I have fulfilled the purpose of a wife. I have given you a son to perpetuate your progeny and also a daughter to give Kanyadanam and get a place in the Heaven. You alone have the capacity to bring up the children among us. But, I can't do it in the absence of any male support. Just like a hawk, people will be waiting to snatch away a left over piece of meat, widows like me in this world. A woman who has lost the support of a husband can do nothing and is a dead weight to the family. So, send me to the demon Bakasura. Sastras say that a woman should not live to be a widow. I am not afraid of death. After me you may get remarried. There is nothing wrong in doing so. So, please send me to the demon unhesitatingly."

The brahmin on hearing these words of his wife began to weep more bitterly than before unable to control the surging sorrow. He said:

"Dear don't talk as you have done so far. To get a good-character cooperative life-partner like you, one must in the past be a very lucky one and must have done good deeds in the past life. It is the duty of every husband to protect his wife. I would be committing the greatest sin if I send you to the demon to be killed and eaten by him."

The daughter of the brahmin who was listening to her parents intervened and said:

"Father! Please listen to me also before you decide. To overcome this dangerous predicament, the only way is to send me to the demon. Then only I die. All the others would survive. Use me as a boat to cross this perilous river of the present situation in our family. If you die, we all become orphans. So, please send me to the demon as his prey on behalf of our family today."

Hearing the words of great sacrifice of their daughter, the Brahmin and his wife could not control the tears surging out of their eyes.

The young boy, though very young still unable to see the plight of his parents, crying, weeping and wailing, went to each of them and shouted:

"Mother and father, don't be afraid of that demon. I shall smash him with this stick!" So saying he picked up a stick placed in the corner of the room. The parents were at a loss either to laugh or cry at the innocence of their young child!

It was at this juncture that Kuntidevi entered the apartment of the brahmin family. She asked them:

"What ails you all? Reveal it to me. I shall try to help you."

"Oh mother! It is not a simple problem you can easily solve. There is a cave near outside our town. There a demon by name Bakasura lives. He is a very strong, wicked and cruel demon. We are all victims of his cruel acts for the last thirteen years. The king of this Kingdom has run away from this place to another far away town Vetrakeeya, unable to protect us from the demon. The demon often invades this town kills persons without

discrimination of young or old or woman or children for his food. We the citizens to avoid the indiscriminate killings by him, entered into an agreement with him not to slay us indiscriminately and in return we agreed to send him everyday the food for him. He requires large quantities of meat, cooked rice, curd and two fat bulls. One member of each family in the town has to take the food to him and that member will also be a part of his food! Today it is our turn to take the food to him. Even the king has failed to protect us from this evil. Who else would come to our rescue? We don't have at least money to hire somebody as a substitute to one member of our family. Rich people in the town are resorting to hiring somebody and thus escape from the calamity they have to face. My conscience does not permit me to send either my wife or my children. Or can I go and leave all these people orphans."

Kuntidevi listened to the brahmin's narration sympathetically, went to her apartment and told Bheemasena how the citizens of the town were suffering on account of the atrocity of the demon and the problem faced by the brahmin's family on that day. Bheemasena agreed to kill the demon Bakasura and relieve the citizens from the perils faced by them. Kuntidevi came back to the apartment of the brahmin family. She told the brahmin:

"You don't worry about your plight. I have five strong sons who are capable of killing the demon. One of my sons will take the food to the demon instead of one member of your family."

"No...no..." protested the brahmin saying:

"No...mother...please don't do it. I cannot commit the great sin of being the cause of the death of one of our guests!

But, Kuntidevi said:

"Oh brahmin! Don't be afraid of any evil consequences to my sons. They have Mantrasakthi and have killed several demons earlier. But, don't reveal our plan to anybody. But, again if you leak out the plan to anybody, my sons would lose their Mantrasakthi."

She told them to keep it a secret lest Duryodhana might come to know about the death of Bakasura and he might suspect that the person who killed him could not be any person other than Bheemasena. If the identity of the Pandavas is revealed by Duryodhana, then the Pandavas have to be in exile for another twelve years!

Bheemasena's joy knew no bounds as he had an opportunity to test his strength.

Dharmaraja and the other brothers returned after completing their begging round. They came to know the Kuntidevi's promise to the brahmin family. Dharmaraja protested to his mother Kuntidevi:

"Oh mother! How did you make the promise without considering the consequences of your action. We are mainly dependent on Bheemasena for our protection, for winning back our lost kingdom we have lost to

Duryodhana and for everything else. Can we afford to sacrifice the life of Bheemasena just to give succour to a brahmin family?"

Kuntidevi replied:

"Son Yudhishtira! You are famous for your observance of Dharma. You are the very incarnation of Dharma. The brahmin family has given us protection during our most difficult times. We are safe, thanks to them. 'Help those who helped us' is the motto of good character and is a moral obligation. It is also our duty. I know the strength of Bheemasena and his capacity to kill the demon Bakasura. Could there be any danger to Bheemasena who killed demons like Hidambasura and others. Let us help the brahmin family and also the citizens of this town who are feeding us!"

Dharmaraja was convinced and blessed Bheemasena.

The citizens of Ekachakranagar came to know this. They all collected huge quantity of meat, cooked rice, curds and two fat bullocks. They placed all the foods in big vessels on the cart.

Bheemasena got on to the cart and drove towards the cave where the demon was waiting for his daily food from the citizens of Ekachakranagar. They all accompanied Bheemasena up to some distance from the cave and waited to see the future happenings.

The demon Bakasura was waiting near the cave for the cart to come. He was angry as the arrival of his food was delayed as Bheemasena spent some time eating away all the food in the cart intended for the demon.

When the demon came to know that Bheemasena had eaten away all the food intended for him, he came running ferociously and attacked him. But, Bheemasena after a brief fight killed the demon Bakasura. He brought the dead body of the demon loaded on the cart for the citizens of Ekachakranagar to see it.

The citizens on seeing the corpse of the demon danced in ecstasy showering praises on their benefactor Bheemasena and his mother Kuntidevi.

12. Ekalavya

This episode from Mahabharata tells us how a young man made a great sacrifice as demanded by his absentia teacher.

Ekalavya was the son of Hiranyadhamya, a hill-tribe king.

Ekalavya was keen to learn and master archery. He came to Dronacharya, an expert in archery, who was giving training to the Pandavas and the Kauravas. He requested him to take him as one of the pupils. Dronacharya refused to take him on the ground that he belonged to a low-caste hill-tribe.

Ekalavya returned to his abode in the forest disappointed but did not give up his ambition. He made a statue of Dronacharya from mud. Treating it as his master in absentia, he worshipped it everyday and began to practise archery. In due course he mastered archery.

One day Pandavas and Kauravas went on a hunting expedition accompanied by hunting dogs. One of the dogs lost the tract and went towards the abode of Ekalavya. The dog on seeing Ekalavya began to bark at him. Ekalavya with seven arrows shut the mouth of the dog without injuring it and causing no pain. The dog returned to the Pandavas. The Pandavas and particularly Arjuna wondered at the extraordinary skill of the archer who had shut the mouth of dog in such a way. They went to Ekalavya and questioned him:

SURA'S ● Supreme Sacrifice and Other Moral Tales from Mahabharata

"Youngman, who are you? Who is your master who gave you the training in archery?"

"My name is Ekalavya and I am the son of the hill-tribe king Hiranyadhamya here. My master is the famous archer Dronacharya!"

The Pandavas and the Kauravas returned to the capital. Arjuna met his Guru Dronacharya and asked him:

"Oh my master! You have been telling everybody that you would make me best archer in the world but you have made one Ekalavya as good an archer as myself or even a better one."

He then told him about the skill exhibited by Ekalavya and his telling that his master was Dronacharya.

Dronacharya and Arjuna then went to Ekalavya. Ekalavya told them how on refusal by Dronacharya to take him as his pupil, he made a statue of Dronacharya and treated it as master-in-absentia and practised archery.

Dronacharya wanted to see that Ekalavya was disabled to use the bow. He asked Ekalavya to give him Gurudakshina (fees) for having treated him as his master.

Ekalavya said:

"O master! I am a poor man. What can I give?"

Dronacharya then asked:

"Give me your right-hand thumb!"

Ekalavya gladly cut his right-hand thumb and presented to Dronacharya. Dronacharya thus removed the rival to his beloved pupil Arjuna in the sport of archery.

13. Sibi Chakravarthi

This episode describes how a king was ready to give away his life to protect a person who sought shelter under him.

Once upon a time there lived a great king called Sibi. He was very kind and charitable and became very famous. His fame spread all over the earth and spread to the heaven too.

The lord of heaven Indra wanted to test and see if the king Sibi was really as great as his fame proclaimed him to be.

So, Indra and god Agni started from heaven. Agni assumed the form of a dove and Indra, of a fierce hawk. Agni flew in the front fluttering the wings as though terrified and Indra followed at a distance as if in hot pursuit. They straight flew to the palace of the king.

Sibi was in the garden distributing charities to the poor. The little fluttering frightened dove came and perched upon the wrist of Sibi looking at him with tearful eyes full of fear. Sibi immediately took her in his hands. Stroking her back kindly, he said, "Fear not, O dove, I will save you from all harm."

Just as he was saying this, the hawk came angrily and tried to snatch the dove away from the king's hands. But, the king raised his hand in a flash and obstructed the hawk. The hawk looked at the king angrily and said speaking like a human being, "This dove is my bird of prey. I had been pursuing it from the morning. Why do you obstruct me in having my food, O king?"

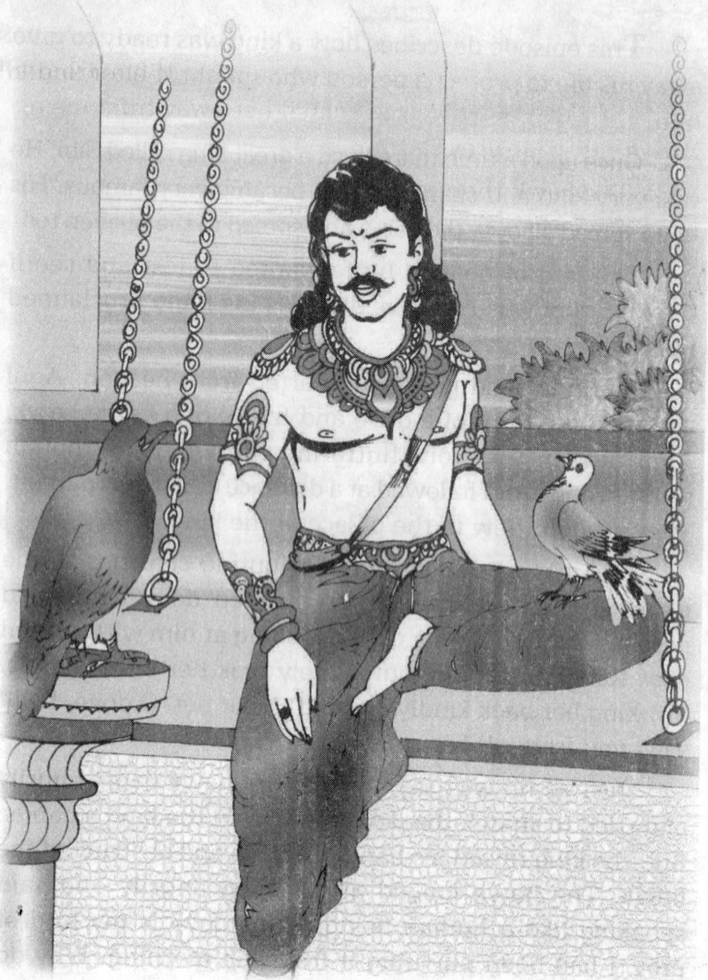

Surprised at hearing the hawk speak like a man, Sibi replied, "I do not know who you are, O hawk, who can thus speak like a man. This poor frightened dove has sought my shelter. It is my duty to protect her from all harm. I won't allow you to snatch her away from me and make her your prey."

The hawk then said, "Rajan, you are renowned as a kind one. Perhaps it is your duty to protect those in distress. But is your kindness limited only to the dove? What about me? Am I not equally entitled to claim your pity? I am a bird who can live only eating the meat of smaller birds. By depriving me of my food are you not condemning me to die? Is this your dharma?"

King Sibi was nonplussed. The hawk could not only speak like a human being but also argue like one! Evidently his duty was towards both the dove and the hawk. He was very thoughtful. At last he said, "Hawk, what you say is true. I won't deprive you of your food. But, at the same time I can't give up this poor frightened dove. Will you accept if I give you some other flesh as a substitute?"

The hawk replied, "Very well king, I have no objection as long as my hunger is satisfied. But, you must give me flesh exactly equal to that of the dove. I won't accept less." And he further mockingly added, "But where do you get substitute flesh from? Will you kill another life to save the life of this dove?"

Sibi hastily replied, "No, no, I won't think of harming another life, be sure. I will give you my own flesh in the place of the dove."

He then turned to his attendants and ordered them to bring a balance. The attendants accordingly brought the balance and erected it before the king. Sibi placed the dove on one side of the balance. He took out his sword and cutting small portions of his flesh placed it on the other side. But strange! The dove which looked so small and frail appeared to grow in weight, and any amount of flesh in the pan could not outbalance it. King Sibi went on cutting portion after portion from his body and placing it in the balance... yet to no purpose.... till at last no more flesh remained in him to cut. Wondering at the heaviness of the dove, Sibi then threw away the sword and himself mounted the balance. Lo, now the balance was quite equal. Rejoicing that he was at last able to give the hawk its due, Sibi turned to the hawk and said, "O hawk, my weight is equal to the weight of the dove. Please eat me and leave the dove."

As he said these words there was a cheering applause from the gods who gathered in the sky to witness the test. They beat the heavenly drums and showered flowers on the king. The hawk and the dove shed their assumed forms and stood before him in their shining glorious forms. Sibi looked at them in blank amazement.

Indra said, "O kindly king, know that we are Indra and Agni come down from heaven to test you. You have indeed proved yourself to be greater than your fame. You will be blessed with long life and vast riches. Your name will remain in the world as long as the sun and moon remain."

SURA'S ● Supreme Sacrifice and Other Moral Tales from Mahabharata

So saying, Indra touched Sibi with his hand. Lo! All the cuts and wounds vanished from Sibi's body and he stood there as strong as ever. He bowed to the gods with great devotion, who blessed him and returned to their abodes.

14. Lord Vishnu Gives Food

Lord Vishnu is the sustainer of the whole world and he feeds all the living beings. Lakshmi Devi is his consort. Daily she waits for him to come home after his work is finished. Everyday the Lord comes very late. One day the Lord was very much delayed. Lakshmi Devi had to wait for him for a long time. She got even tired, while waiting for him. While the Lord was taking food, she asked, "Oh Lord! Why do you come so late? Why don't you come a little early hereafter?"

Sri Mahavishnu looked at her and smiled, "Devi, don't you know how busy I am? There are millions and millions of living beings on earth and day by day the number is going up. I have to feed all of them before I can think of eating."

Lakshmi Devi opened her eyes wide in astonishment. "Have you to feed all of them personally everyday? Don't you ever forget anyone?"

The Lord shook his head and said, "No, how can I forget anyone? According to each one's prarabdha, I have to supply food everyday. This is a must."

"Really!" thought Lakshmi Devi within herself, "I must test my husband one day and see whether he is as diligent as he claims to be."

SURA'S ● Supreme Sacrifice and Other Moral Tales from Mahabharata

103

The next day she caught hold of a tiny ant and kept in a small box. She put the box inside the almyrah and waited to see when the Lord would feed the ant. As usual the Lord came late in the afternoon looking very tired and hungry. Lakshmi Devi served the food and while the Lord was eating, she asked:

"My Lord, have you fed all the beings today?"

The Lord nodded his head indicating that he did so.

Lakshmi Devi laughed and said, "No Darling, today you forgot at least one being."

Sri Mahavishnu raised his eyebrows and exclaimed, "I forget somebody? Never."

Lakshmi Devi smiled and brought out the box from the almyrah.

"See, I kept an ant here in the morning. You never came near the box and fed the ant. I had been watching the almyrah from the morning.

"Lord Vishnu thunderously laughed and replied, "My dear, open up the box and see whether the ant has its food or not."

In surprise Lakshmi Devi opened the box. There, the ant had a bit of jaggery in its mouth. Lakshmi Devi understood that the Lord takes care of all and forgets none.

15. Dharmavyadha

This episode tells the tale of a person who served his old parents and carried his caste profession honestly. Kausika was a very learned Brahmin. He had mastered all the Vedas and Sastras. He used to earn his livelihood by begging. But, he was conceited. One day while he was doing penance under a tree, a Crane excreted from the tree on him. He enraged looked at the Crane with fierce eyes. The Crane was burnt to ashes.

He then went to a house and stood before it and called for alms. The housewife was about to bring alms when her husband came to the house. As a dutiful and devoted wife, she followed her husband to look after his immediate needs and serve him food. After that she came and gave alms to the brahmin. The brahmin annoyed at the delay and looked at her angrily with fierce eyes. She told him:

"O brahmin! for a woman, there is no greater god than her husband. Any other work will be done only after attending to his needs first. Did you think I am a Crane to get burnt from your fierce looks? If you still want to learn about dharmasutras go and meet a butcher by name Dharmavyadha in the city of Mithila."

Kausika went to Mithila, located the house of Dharmavyadha. He was selling goat meat and poke. Dharmavyadha saw Kausika standing at a distance in front of his shop. He approached Kausika and said:

"You are a sacred brahmin. Our regards to the Pathivratha Siromani woman who directed you to me!"

Kausika was surprised how he knew all about his visit to the house of the woman without his disclosing it.

He took the brahmin to his house, treated him with all hospitality due to a brahmin and said:

"Serving my old parents and extending due hospitality to guests, I am carrying on with my caste trade (Swadharma) with honesty. I take my food only after all those depending on me take their food. To carry on one's caste-trade with honesty is everybody's duty. In our country a father meets justice to his own erring son even. Nonviolence and truth-speaking lifts a man to a higher status. You may ask me if I am not guilty of violence in killing animals for my trade! But, every living being is dependent on every other living being for its living! Is there no life in the vegetables you eat? Killing for the sake of earning food from it, is no violence. This is Dharma. I have acquired all this knowledge by serving my old parents. Service to parents is my only penance."

Kausika enlightened by Dharmavyadha felt ashamed of his conceit.